INSPIRE

HAIR FASHION FOR SALON CLIENTS

Salon Fluxx • HAIR: Liza Espinoza • MAKEUP: Kelli Kolors • PHOTO: Steven Ledell

INSPIRE
HAIR FASHION FOR SALON CLIENTS
Featuring TEXTURES

Table of Contents Volume 72

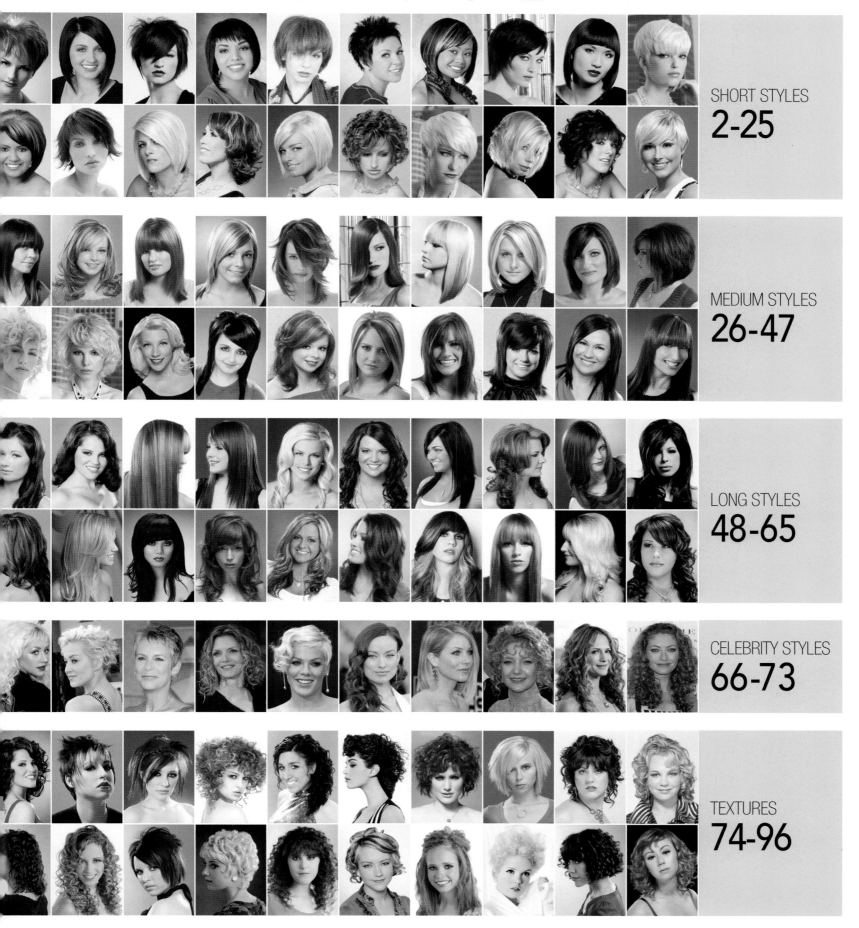

Casal's de Spa & Salon
HAIR: Sara Beech
PHOTO: Tom Carson

PON International
HAIR: Pon Saradeth
MAKEUP: Jamie Queenin
PHOTO: Taggart Winterhalter
for Purely Visual

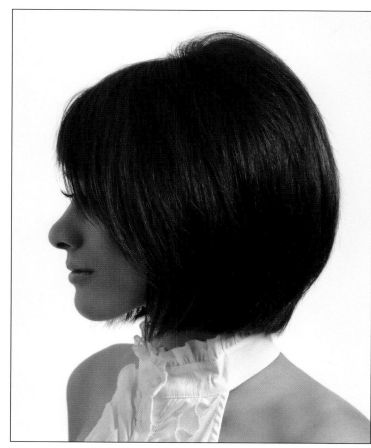

Fantastic Sams
Foothill Ranch, CA
HAIR: Charles Holdeman
PHOTO: Taggart Winterhalter
for Purely Visual

Tangles Salon
HAIR: Michelle Azouz
PHOTO: Tom Carson

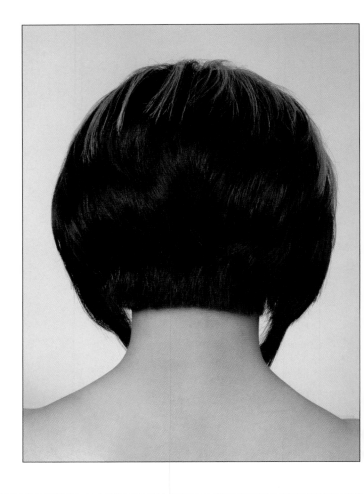

Fantastic Sams-Corona, CA
HAIR: Guadalupe Mariscal
PHOTO: Taggart Winterhalter
for Purely Visual

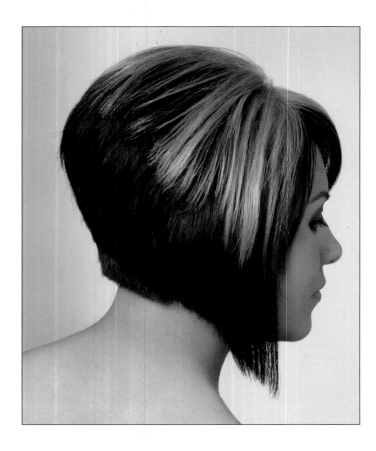

ENJOY Professional Hair Care
HAIR: Vincent Michael
COLOR: Tawny Pierce
MAKEUP: Sara Wayne
PHOTO: Taggart Winterhalter
for Purely Visual

The Brown Aveda Institute
HAIR: Megan Anderson
PHOTO: Tom Carson

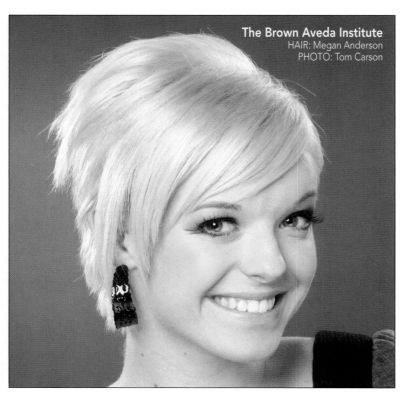

Tangles Salon
HAIR: Leslie Cook
PHOTO: Tom Carson

Kathy Adams Salon
HAIR: Lauren Houser
MAKEUP: Rachael Jacobsen
PHOTO: Tom Carson

Diadema Hair Fashion
HAIR: Diadema
MAKEUP: Cristina Marzo per 20100Milano
PHOTO: Stefano Bidini

Shortino's Salon & Day Spa
HAIR: Shortino's Salon & Day Spa
PHOTO: Tom Carson

Fantastic Sams-Corona, CA
HAIR: Karina Cortez
PHOTO: Taggart Winterhalter
for Purely Visual

PON International
HAIR: Stacy Burdge
MAKEUP: Jamie Queenin
PHOTO: Taggart Winterhalter
for Purely Visual

Fantastic Sams-Corona, CA
HAIR: Patti Mead
PHOTO: Taggart Winterhalter for
Purely Visual

A Touch of Class
HAIR: Frank Marasco
COLOR: A Touch of Class Team of
Professional Colorists
MAKEUP: Louise Boyd &
Amy Gravelle
PHOTO: Frank Marasco

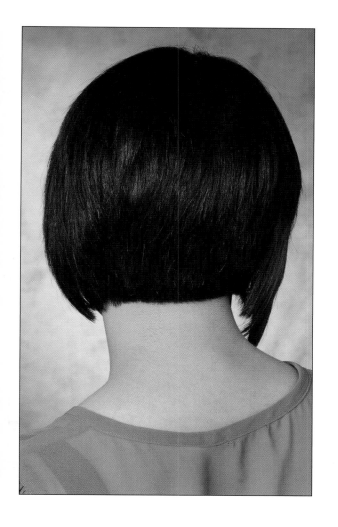

Fantastic Sams-Corona, CA
HAIR: Anna Reyes
PHOTO: Taggart Winterhalter
for Purely Visual

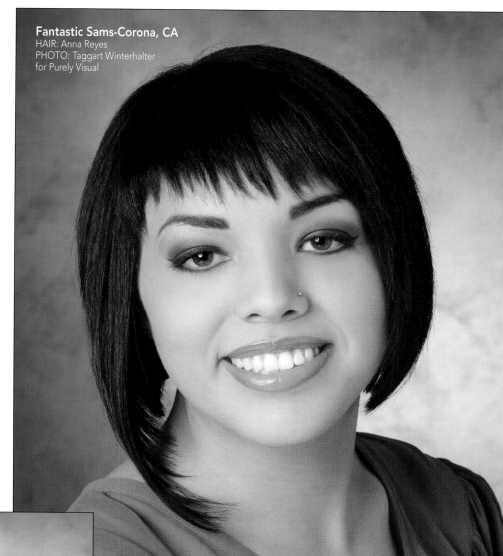

Pivot Point International
HAIR: Joakim Roos
MAKEUP: Dino
PHOTO: Mike van den Toorn/Tina Rayyan

Shortino's Salon & Day Spa
HAIR: Shortino's Salon & Day Spa
PHOTO: Tom Carson

Diadema Hair Fashion
HAIR: Diadema
MAKEUP: Cristina Marzo
per 20100Milano
PHOTO: Stefano Bidini

The David Salon
HAIR: Nicole Ankenman
MAKEUP: Jen Harklerode
PHOTO: Taggart Winterhalter
for Purely Visual

ENJOY Professional Hair Care
HAIR: Nick Flier
COLOR: Araz Sinblian
MAKEUP: Sara Wayne
PHOTO: Taggart Winterhalter
for Purely Visual

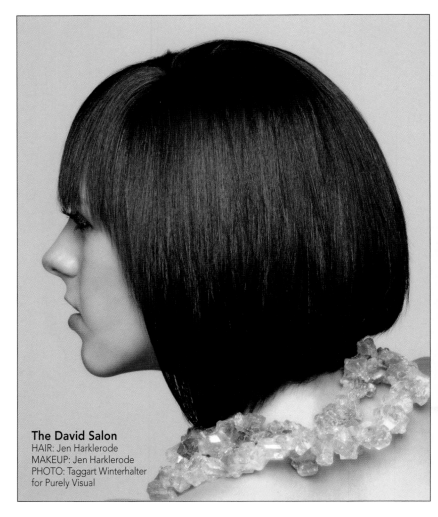

The David Salon
HAIR: Jen Harklerode
MAKEUP: Jen Harklerode
PHOTO: Taggart Winterhalter
for Purely Visual

ColorWorks
HAIR: Tracy Guthrie
MAKEUP: Craig D.Miller
PHOTO: Taggart Winterhalter
for Purely Visual

19

The Brown Aveda Institute
Rocky River, OH
HAIR: Rosa Lee
PHOTO: Tom Carson

The Brown Aveda Institute
Rocky River, OH
HAIR: Kayla Hofer
PHOTO: Tom Carson

Pivit Point Finland
HAIR: Marja Rahikainen
MAKEUP: Dino
PHOTO: Mike van den Toorn

The Ohio Academy
Paul Mitchell Partner School
Columbus, OH
HAIR: Jessica Russo
MAKEUP: Chloe Gomez
PHOTO: Tom Carson

The Ohio Academy
Paul Mitchell Partner School
Twinsburg, OH
HAIR: Alli Radesic
PHOTO: Tom Carson

21

Diadema Hair Fashion
HAIR: Diadema
MAKEUP: Cristina Marzo
per 20100Milano
PHOTO: Stefano Bidini

**The Ohio Academy
Paul Mitchell
Partner School
Twinsburg, OH**
HAIR: Alli Radesic
PHOTO: Tom Carson

The David Salon
HAIR:Kristine Agrusa
MAKEUP: Diane Davis
PHOTO: Taggart Winterhalter
for Purely Visual

Shortino's Salon & Day Spa
HAIR: Shortino's Salon & Day Spa
PHOTO: Tom Carson

Kathy Adams Salon
HAIR: Michelle Plummer
MAKEUP: Melissa McDonald
PHOTO: Tom Carson

Kathy Adams Salon
HAIR: Arica Diaz
MAKEUP: Melissa McDonald
PHOTO: Tom Carson

Scruples Professional
Salon Products, Inc.
HAIR: Terrence Renk
MAKEUP: Ronda Jackson
PHOTO: Jake Armor

The Brown Aveda Institute
HAIR: Alexis Coduti
PHOTO: Tom Carson

The Brown Aveda Institute
Rocky River, OH
HAIR: E.J. Baire & Colby Sprague
PHOTO: Tom Carson

28

Oak Street Hair Group
HAIR: Scott Thomason
MAKEUP: Angela Jones
PHOTO: Tom Carson

The Brown Aveda Institute
HAIR: Julie Jasinski
PHOTO: Tom Carson

Alexander's Grand Salon & Spa
HAIR: Lori Kurtz
MAKEUP: Amy Kaniewski-Clemons
PHOTO: Taggart Winterhalter for Purely Visual

Shortino's Salon & Day Spa
HAIR: Shortino's Salon & Day Spa
PHOTO: Tom Carson

Tangles Salon
HAIR: Salina Bernal
PHOTO: Tom Carson

Tangles Salon
HAIR: Salina Bernal
PHOTO: Tom Carson

Jesse Daniel Salon
HAIR: Tami Fleming
MAKEUP: Jamie Queenin
PHOTO: Taggart Winterhalter
for Purely Visual

Pivot Point International
HAIR: Sven Ewald
MAKEUP: Dino
PHOTO: Mike van den Toorn/Tina Rayyan

The Ohio Academy
Paul Mitchell Partner School
HAIR: Alishia West Steigerwald
PHOTO: Tom Carson

Tangles Salon
HAIR: Chase Williams
PHOTO: Tom Carson

Casal's de Spa & Salon
HAIR: Katie Ponko
MAKEUP: Tia Makosky
PHOTO: Tom Carson

Fantastic Sams-Corona, CA
HAIR: Eneyda Puente
PHOTO: Taggart Winterhalter
for Purely Visual

PON International
HAIR: Kaytee Varchetto
MAKEUP: Sara Wayne
PHOTO: Taggart
Winterhalter for
Purely Visual

Tangles Salon
HAIR: Robin Cook
PHOTO: Tom Carson

Casal's de Spa & Salon
HAIR: Deiree Gabriel
MAKEUP: Carrie Decesare
PHOTO: Tom Carson

ColorWorks
HAIR: Tracy Guthrie
MAKEUP: Craig D.Miller
PHOTO: Taggart Winterhalter for Purely Visual

PON International
HAIR: Pon Saradeth
MAKEUP: Jamie Queenin
PHOTO: Taggart Winterhalter
for Purely Visual

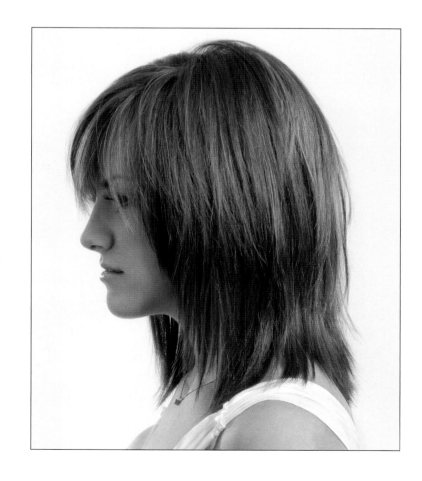

PON International
HAIR: Todd Snow
MAKEUP: Jamie Queenin
PHOTO: Taggart Winterhalter
for Purely Visual

The Ohio Academy
Paul Mitchell Partner School
Twinsburg, OH
HAIR: Janine Widrich
PHOTO: Tom Carson

40

**The Brown Aveda Institute
Rocky River, OH**
HAIR: Kristen Weber
PHOTO: Tom Carson

Bella Fiore Hair Salon
HAIR: Shelley Prince
PHOTO: Kevin Meyers

The Ohio Academy
Paul Mitchell Partner School
Twinsburg, OH
HAIR: Sarah Dougherty
PHOTO: Tom Carson

The Ohio Academy
Paul Mitchell Partner School
Twinsburg, OH
HAIR: Katie Good
PHOTO: Tom Carson

Diadema Hair Fashion
HAIR: Diadema
MAKEUP: Cristina Marzo
per 20100Milano
PHOTO: Stefano Bidini

Alexander's Grand Salon & Spa
HAIR: Malorie Briley
MAKEUP: Amy Kaniewski-Clemons
PHOTO: Taggart Winterhalter
for Purely Visual

élon Salon
HAIR: Michelle Metz
COLOR: Natalia Starks
MAKEUP: Fawn Ortega
PHOTO: Scott Bryant
Art Directon by Larry Oskin
& The Marketing
Solutions Team

44

The Brown Aveda Institute
HAIR: Dijana Smiljanic
PHOTO: Tom Carson

Cloud 9 Salon
HAIR: Kenyetta Green
MAKEUP: Angie Mamone
PHOTO: Tom Carson

Diadema Hair Fashion
HAIR: Diadema
MAKEUP: Cristina Marzo
per 20100 Milano
PHOTO: Stefano Bidini

Kathy Adams Salon
HAIR: Kathy McCaffrey
MAKEUP: Melissa McDonald
PHOTO: Tom Carson

Kathy Adams Salon
HAIR: Dalia Ardev
MAKEUP: Melissa McDonald
PHOTO: Tom Carson

The Brown Aveda Institute
Rocky River, OH
HAIR: Kate Tomaszewski
PHOTO: Tom Carson

Savvy Salon & Spa
HAIR: Pat Helmandollar
MAKEUP: Ashley Brown
PHOTO: Tom Carson

Tangles Salon
HAIR: Keely Martinez
PHOTO: Tom Carson

Salon Fluxx
HAIR: Liza Espinoza
MAKEUP: Krystyn James
PHOTO: Steven Ledell

The Brown Aveda Institute
HAIR: Grace Venman
PHOTO: Tom Carson

Fantastic Sams-Corona, CA
HAIR: Magda Zapien
PHOTO: Taggart Winterhalter
for Purely Visual

Octagon Spa & Salon
HAIR: Bianca Reed/Divina Luna
COLOR: Bianca Reed
MAKEUP: Bianca Reed
PHOTO: Eric Peterson

ENJOY Professional Hair Care
HAIR: Donny Anderson
COLOR: Bobby Paul
MAKEUP: Sara Wayne
PHOTO: Taggart Winterhalter
for Purely Visual

Tantrum Salon
HAIR: Albert Cortez
MAKEUP: Sara Wayne
PHOTO: Taggart Winterhalter
for Purely Visual

Kathy Adams Salon
HAIR: Kathy McCaffrey
MAKEUP: Lauren Muncher
PHOTO: Tom Carson

Kathy Adams Salon
HAIR: Kathy McCaffrey
MAKEUP: Lauren Muncher
PHOTO: Tom Carson

AG Hair Cosmetics
HAIR: Artistic Director, Jami Symons:
Artistic Team Leader, Jo-Anne Dicken;
Artistic Team Member, Jaclyn Emmett
MAKEUP: Yasaman Morshedian
PHOTO: Waldy Martens

The Brown Aveda Institute
HAIR: Shawna Lipstrev
PHOTO: Tom Carson

The Brown Aveda Institute
Rocky River, OH
HAIR: Caitlin Whitney & Christin Ryan
PHOTO: Tom Carson

Fantastic Sams-
Huntington Beach, CA
HAIR: Jennifer Newman
PHOTO: Taggart Winterhalter
for Purely Visual

Tangles Salon
HAIR: Leslie Cook
PHOTO: Tom Carson

Kathy Adams Salon
HAIR: Cindy Freeze
MAKEUP: Cindy Freeze
PHOTO: Tom Carson

Irvin's Salon
HAIR: LaShaundra "Shauney" Harris
Jessica Hayes
MAKEUP: Michelle Aristocrat
PHOTO: Rodney Davenport LIT Photography

**Fantastic Sams-
Huntington Beach, CA**
HAIR: Elizabeth Strohecker
PHOTO: Taggart Winterhalter
for Purely Visual

AG Hair Cosmetics
HAIR: Artistic Director, Jami Symons:
Artistic Team Leader, Jo-Anne Dicken;
Artistic Team Member, Jaclyn Emmett
MAKEUP: Yasaman Morshedian
PHOTO: Waldy Martens

The Brown Aveda Institute
HAIR: Lauryn Mesojedec
& Katherine Andrasak
PHOTO: Tom Carson

Kathy Adams Salon
HAIR: Hillary Pratt
MAKEUP: Melissa McDonald
PHOTO: Tom Carson

Tangles Salon
HAIR: Chase Williams
PHOTO: Tom Carson

Tangles Salon
HAIR: Dora Guerrero
PHOTO: Tom Carson

**The Ohio Academy
Paul Mitchell Partner School
Columbus, OH**
HAIR: Julie Adrian
MAKEUP: Amanda Morris
PHOTO: Tom Carson

Fantastic Sams-Murrieta,CA
HAIR: Martha Rosales
PHOTO: Taggart Winterhalter
for Purely Visual

Casal's de Spa & Salon
HAIR: Connie McKinney & Tracy Tedesco
MAKEUP: Melanie McCormick
PHOTO: Tom Carson

Ladies & Gentlemen Salon & Spa
HAIR: Mike Pavlick, Jen Roskey,
Holly Brown & Jen Snyder
MAKEUP: Amy Hoegler
PHOTO: Tom Carson

Olivia Wilde
PHOTO: Jon Kopaloff / FilmMagic

Drew Barrymore
PHOTO: Jeffrey Mayer /
WireImage

Rebecca Gayheart
PHOTO: Gregg DeGuire
WireImage

Anne Heche
PHOTO: Gregg DeGuire /
WireImage

Minnie Driver
PHOTO: Mark Mainz
Getty Images

Christina Applegate
PHOTO: Gregg DeGuire / WireImage

Elizabeth Perkins
PHOTO: Dan MacMedan / WireImage

Elizabeth Perkins
PHOTO: Jeffrey Mayer / WireImage

Jamie Lee Curtis
PHOTO: Jason LaVeris/
FilmMagic

Kellie Pickler
PHOTO: Kevin Mazur /
WireImage

Pink
PHOTO: Frederick M. Brown / Getty Images

Pink
PHOTO: Jon Kopaloff / FilmMagic

Kate Hudson
PHOTO: Steve Granitz / WireImage

Kelly Osbourne
PHOTO: Jason LaVeris / FilmMagic

Faith Hill
PHOTO: Stephen Lovekin /
Getty Images

Michelle Pfeiffer
PHOTO: Sean Gallup /
Getty Images

Michelle Pfeiffer
PHOTO: Pascal Le Segretain / Getty Images

Mary-Louise Parker
PHOTO: Jason LaVeris /
FilmMagic

Mary-Louise Parker
PHOTO: Frazer Harrison /
Getty Images

Holly Hunter
PHOTO: Carlo Allegri /
Getty Images

Christina Aguilera
PHOTO: Kristian Dowling /
Getty Images

AG Hair Cosmetics
HAIR: Artistic Director, Jami Symons:
Artistic Team Leader, Jo-Anne Dicken
Artistic Team Member, Jaclyn Emmett
MAKEUP: Yasaman Morshedian
PHOTO: Waldy Martens

Tangles Salon
HAIR: Robin Cook
PHOTO: Tom Carson

Elie.Elie Salon
HAIR: Barbara Lhoten
MAKEUP: David Maderich
PHOTO: Roberto Ligresti

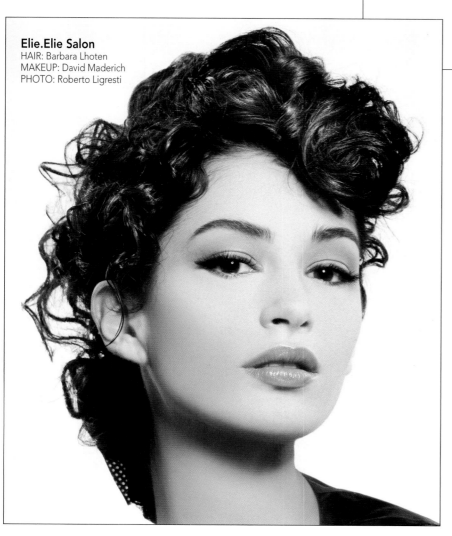

75

Tangles Salon
HAIR: Lesllie Cook
MAKEUP: Betty Mekonnen
PHOTO: Tom Carson

Tantrum Salon
HAIR: Vanessa Lujan
MAKEUP: Jamie Queenin
PHOTO: Taggart Winterhalter
for Purely Visual

The Brown Aveda Institute Rocky River, OH
HAIR: Katherine Adkins & Myrna Christensen
PHOTO: Tom Carson

Fantastic Sams-Corona, CA
HAIR: Shelly Whitaker
PHOTO: Taggart Winterhalter for Purely Visual

Tangles Salon
HAIR: Leslie Cook
PHOTO: Tom Carson

Tangles Salon
HAIR: Michelle Azouz
PHOTO: Tom Carson

80

ColorWorks
HAIR: Tracy Guthrie
MAKEUP: Craig D.Miller
PHOTO: Taggart Winterhalter
for Purely Visual

Tantrum Salon
HAIR: Shannon Trae Johnson
MAKEUP: Sara Wayne
PHOTO: Taggart Winterhalter
for Purely Visual

Tantrum Salon
HAIR: Robert Moreno
MAKEUP: Jamie Queenin
PHOTO: Taggart Winterhalter
for Purely Visual

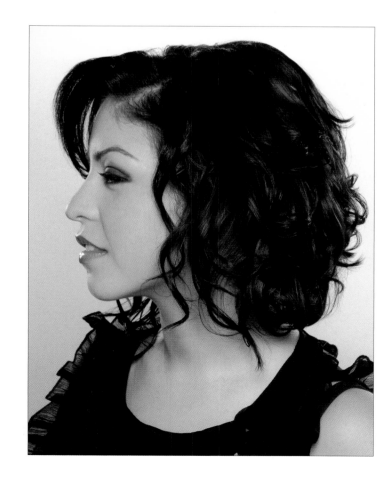

Tantrum Salon
HAIR: Erik Guterrez
MAKEUP: Sara Wayne
PHOTO: Taggart Winterhalter
for Purely Visual

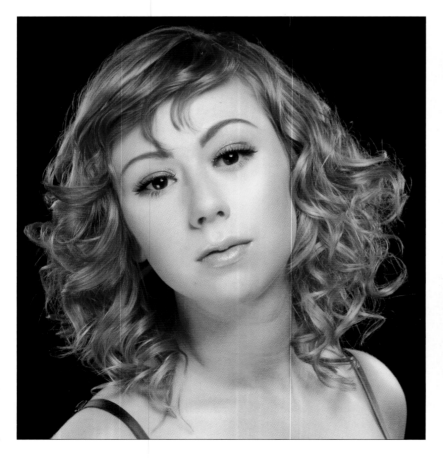

Tangles Salon
HAIR: Michelle Azouz
PHOTO: Tom Carson

Anása Hair Studio
HAIR: Alisha Domasig
MAKEUP: Jamie Queenin
PHOTO: Taggart Winterhalter
for Purely Visual

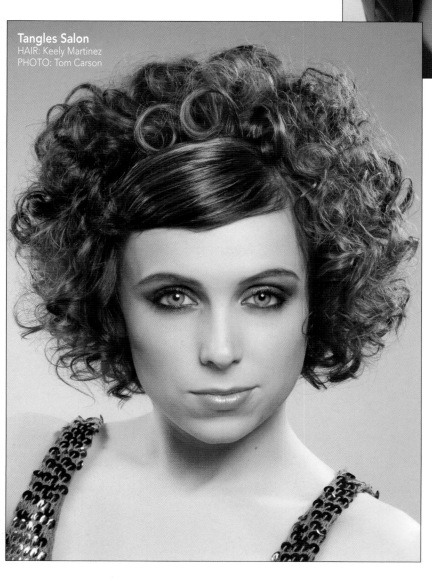

Tangles Salon
HAIR: Keely Martinez
PHOTO: Tom Carson

ColorWorks
HAIR: Tracy Guthrie
MAKEUP: Craig D.Miller
PHOTO: Taggart Winterhalter
for Purely Visual

86

Shortino's Salon & Day Spa
HAIR: Shortino's Salon & Day Spa
PHOTO: Tom Carson

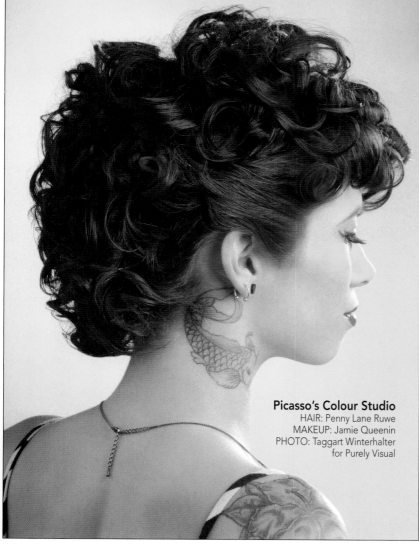

Picasso's Colour Studio
HAIR: Penny Lane Ruwe
MAKEUP: Jamie Queenin
PHOTO: Taggart Winterhalter
for Purely Visual

87

Art of Hair
HAIR: Nicole Martin
MAKEUP: Sara Wayne
PHOTO: Taggart Winterhalter
for Purely Visual

**The Ohio Academy
Paul Mitchell
Partner School
Columbus, OH**
HAIR: Cait Ogilbee
MAKEUP: Chloe Gomez
PHOTO: Tom Carson

élon Salon
HAIR: Ray Brookshire
COLOR: Ray Brookshire
MAKEUP: Fawn/Mac
PHOTO: Scott Bryant
Art Direction by
Larry Oskin &
The Marketing
Solutions Team

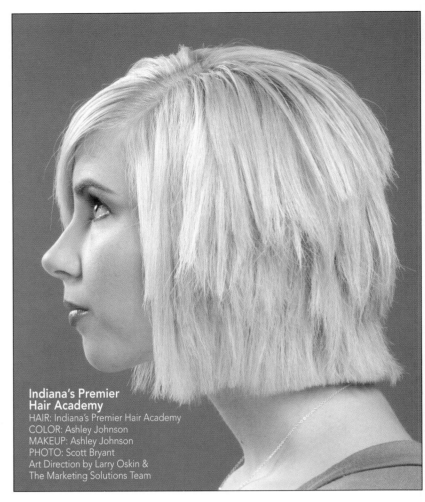

**Indiana's Premier
Hair Academy**
HAIR: Indiana's Premier Hair Academy
COLOR: Ashley Johnson
MAKEUP: Ashley Johnson
PHOTO: Scott Bryant
Art Direction by Larry Oskin &
The Marketing Solutions Team

ColorWorks
HAIR: Tracy Guthrie
MAKEUP: Craig D.Miller
PHOTO: Taggart Winterhalter
for Purely Visual

Picasso's Colour Studio
HAIR: Cynthia Bleier
MAKEUP: Sara Wayne
PHOTO: Taggart Winterhalter
for Purely Visual

Anása Hair Studio
HAIR: Helen Botsis
MAKEUP: Sara Wayne
PHOTO: Taggart Winterhalter
for Purely Visual

Octagon Spa & Salon
HAIR: Sophia Melendez/Vicki Millard
COLOR: Vicki Millard
MAKEUP: Bianca Reed
PHOTO: Eric Peterson

**John Amico Haircare &
Jalyd Haircolor
David The Salon**
HAIR: Abigail Sickman
COLOR: Abigail Sickman
MAKEUP: Abigail Sickman
PHOTO: Scott Bryant
Art Direction by
Larry Oskin &
The Marketing
Solutions Team

Anása Hair Studio
HAIR: Alisha Domasig
MAKEUP: Jeanne Romano
PHOTO: Taggart Winterhalter
for Purely Visual

Luca Bella Salon and Spa
HAIR: Jolene Phillips
MAKEUP: Sara Wayne
PHOTO: Taggart Winterhalter
for Purely Visual

Anása Hair Studio
HAIR: Alisha Domasig
MAKEUP: Jeanne Romano
PHOTO: Taggart Winterhalter
for Purely Visual

Art of Hair
HAIR: Nicole Martin
MAKEUP: Jamie Queenin
PHOTO: Taggart Winterhalter
for Purely Visual

Art of Hair
HAIR: Nicole Martin
MAKEUP: Jamie Queenin
PHOTO: Taggart Winterhalter
for Purely Visual

The Art of Hair Salon
HAIR: Michelle Whinna
MAKEUP: Derya Fejzula
PHOTO: Ray Lasky

Salon Dé Dawn
HAIR: Dawn Orlow Townsend
MAKEUP: Jamie Queenin
PHOTO: Taggart Winterhalter
for Purely Visual

Publisher/CEO: Deborah Carver • Managing Director: Sheryl Lenzkes • Art Director: Michael Block
To Contact Us: Creative Age Communications • 7628 Densmore Avenue, Van Nuys, California 91406-2042 • PH 800.634.8500 • FAX 818.782.7450
Interested in getting published . . . go to inspirebooks.com to download submission forms and information